OKLAHOMA

in words and pictures

BY DENNIS B. FRADIN

ILLUSTRATIONS BY RICHARD WAHL

MAPS BY LEN W. MEENTS

Consultant
    John Heisch
    Head Librarian
    Oklahoma Historical Society

CHILDRENS PRESS ®

CHICAGO

For Elizabeth Stein

For their help, the author thanks:

Ruby Cozad, a Kiowa-Caddo Indian who is also the Administrative
Assistant for Health and Education at the Oklahoma Indian Affairs
Commission

Rain Vehik, Anthropology Department, University of Oklahoma

L.B. McClure, County Agricultural Extension Director of Oklahoma County

Linda Fanselau, Assistant Librarian, Oklahoma Historical Society

A view of the Wichita Mountains from Mt. Scott

Library of Congress Cataloging in Publication Data

Fradin, Dennis B
  Oklahoma in words and pictures.

  SUMMARY: A brief introduction to the history,
geography, industries, cities, tourist attractions,
and famous citizens of Oklahoma, the state that
has more Indians than any other state.
  1. Oklahoma—Juvenile literature. [1. Oklahoma]
I. Wahl, Richard, 1939- II. Meents, Len W.
III. Title.
F694.3.F7   976.6   80-26961
ISBN 0-516-03936-9

Picture Acknowledgments
JAMES P. ROWAN—2, 5, 15, 33 (left)
OKLAHOMA TOURISM AND RECREATION DEPARTMENT PHOTO—9
(top left), 14, 28
OKLAHOMA TOURISM AND RECREATION DEPARTMENT PHOTO BY
FRED W. MARVEL— cover, 9 (bottom left and right), 10, 13, 17, 18, 21,
23, 25 (left), 27 (top right and bottom left), 29, 31, 32, 33 (right), 34, 35,
36, 37, 38, 39, 40, 41, 42
NATIONAL COWBOY HALL OF FAME—22
CHEROKEE NATIONAL HISTORICAL SOCIETY—27 (top left and
bottom right)
COVER PICTURE—No Man's Land Pioneer Day Celebration

Oklahoma

Oklahoma lies in the south-central United States. The word *Oklahoma* comes from the Choctaw (CHOK • taw) Indian language. It means *land of the red people.* The Indian people have played a big role in Oklahoma's history. Once, Indians hunted buffalo in Oklahoma. In the 1800s, the U.S. government drove many Indian tribes into Oklahoma. Today, Oklahoma has more Indians than any other state.

Oklahoma is one of the top oil-producing states. It is a leading state for growing wheat. It also ranks high for raising cattle. Oklahoma's forests, mountains, and lakes make it a lovely state.

Do you know where 50,000 people came to live in one day in 1889? And where another 100,000 came to live in a single day in 1893? Do you know where baseball star Mickey Mantle was born? Or where one of the greatest athletes of all time — Jim Thorpe — was born?

You've probably guessed that the answer to all these questions is: Oklahoma!

Millions of years ago there were no people in Oklahoma. Dinosaurs roamed about. Brontosaurus was there. He ate plants. Allosaurus was there, too. He ate other dinosaurs. Dinosaurs died out long ago. But their bones have been found in Oklahoma. Mammoths and mastodons also lived in Oklahoma. They looked like hairy elephants.

People first came to Oklahoma at least 9,000 years ago. The earliest ones hunted mammoths. They also gathered nuts and plants. Their stone arrowheads have been found in Oklahoma.

Caddo houses

Long before white people settled there, many Indian tribes lived and hunted in Oklahoma. The Osage (oh • SAYJ), Kiowa (KI • oh • wah), Comanche (ko • MAN • chee), Arapaho (ah • RAP • ah • hoe), Wichita (WICH • eh • tah), and Caddo (KAD • oh) were six of the tribes. Many of the Indians hunted buffalo. They ate the meat. They made clothes out of the buffalo skins. Some Oklahoma Indians also farmed. Corn, squash, and beans were three of their main crops. While hunting, Indians often lived in tents called *tepees*. Some who farmed built permanent houses out of poles, twigs, and grass.

Spanish explorers were the first non-Indians in Oklahoma. In the 1500s stories were told about "cities of gold" in America. These cities were said to have streets and houses of gold. In 1540 the Spanish explorer Coronado began a long search for gold. In 1541 his trip took him through Oklahoma. Coronado didn't find gold there. Neither did other Spanish explorers. Spain lost interest in Oklahoma.

In 1682 the explorer La Salle claimed a huge piece of land for France. Oklahoma was included. A few French fur traders arrived. But France, like Spain, had little interest in Oklahoma.

In 1776 a new country was formed in America. This was the United States of America. In 1803, by the Louisiana Purchase, the United States bought a huge piece of land from France. Oklahoma was part of this land.

In the early 1800s many American settlers moved into Alabama, Georgia, and the rest of the southeastern United States. As this happened, the Indians were pushed off their lands. Sometimes the Indians were beaten in fights. Other times they were cheated out of their homelands. Still other times they were just told to leave. The United States government looked for a place to send Choctaw, Creek, Chickasaw (CHICK • ah • saw), Cherokee, and Seminole (SEM • eh • nole) Indians. Oklahoma was picked.

Starting in the 1820s, thousands of these Indians were sent to Oklahoma. Often, they had to walk there. Some who would not move were sent in chains. The Indians didn't have enough clothing or blankets. They had to walk barefoot over snow. Many died on the way. The Indians named these trips the "Trail of Tears."

The Indians of Oklahoma hold some colorful celebrations. Some of them are Choctaw dancing (above left), the Cherokee National Holiday (above right), and the Pawnee homecoming (left).

Oklahoma land was given to each of these five tribes. The Indians feared losing these new lands, just as they had lost their old homes. The U.S. government said that this wouldn't happen. The Indians were promised their Oklahoma lands for "as long as grass shall grow and rivers run." In fact, the name for Oklahoma at this time was *Indian Territory*.

A statue of Sequoya at the American Indian Hall of Fame

The Indians set up farms and ranches. They built churches and schools. They had their own capital cities, lawmakers, and courts. The Cherokee leader Sequoya (seh • KWOI • ah) had developed a written alphabet for his people. The Cherokee were taught to read and write in their language. In 1844 the Cherokee printed Oklahoma's first newspaper. It was called the *Cherokee Advocate.* Oklahoma Indians had such an advanced way of life that they were called the "Five Civilized Tribes."

In 1861 war started between the Northern and Southern states. This was called the Civil War. Many Oklahoma Indians wanted to have nothing to do with the fighting. But some owned slaves, like other Southerners. Such Indians often fought for the South.

The South lost the Civil War in 1865. The United States government punished Oklahoma Indians for fighting on the Southern side. The Indians had to give up some of their lands in the west. Other Indian tribes were sent to live there.

After the Civil War, cattlemen drove cattle between Texas and Kansas. They passed through Oklahoma. Sometimes the cattlemen paid the Indians for the right to pass through their lands. Other times they just did it without asking.

White farmers also had their eyes on the Indians' lands. A group known as the "Boomers" broke the law by moving there. Again and again, government soldiers threw the Boomers out.

Finally, in 1889 the U.S. government bought some land from the Creek and the Seminole. The government said that white settlers could move onto this land. But the settlers couldn't move there until noon of April 22, 1889.

In April of 1889 people gathered at the borders of what was called the Unassigned Lands. At noon of April 22, cannons were to be fired. Then people could race as fast as they wanted into the Unassigned Lands. To claim 160 acres, a person just had to put down a stake.

Soldiers were stationed to keep people from entering the area before noon. But some sneaked in before the signal was given. These people were called "Sooners," because they arrived too soon. Many of the Sooners were caught and wound up with no land at all.

At noon of April 22, 1889 the cannons were fired. The race was on. People on horses, in wagons, and on foot raced to claim the best lands. Some even came by train. They jumped off when they saw land they liked. On this

Oklahoma remembers the early settlers with statues of the 89ers (above left) and Pioneer Woman (above) and with an 89er day celebration in Guthrie (left).

one day, about 50,000 settlers arrived in Oklahoma. Before the day ended Oklahoma City, Guthrie (GUTH • ree), and Norman were founded.

Some Oklahoma settlers cut up chunks of the ground into bricks. By piling up these bricks, they made what were called *sod* houses. Other settlers built log houses. The settlers planted corn, wheat, and cotton. They built schools and churches in their growing towns.

The Wichita Mountains Wildlife Refuge

In 1890 the U.S. government created the Territory of Oklahoma. What is now the state of Oklahoma then had two parts. There was Indian Territory in the east. There was the Oklahoma Territory with its white settlers to the west. The two were called the "Twin Territories."

During the 1890s the Indians sold more of their lands. There were more "runs," in which settlers claimed homesteads. The greatest one was in 1893. On September 16 of that year, over 100,000 settlers arrived.

Texas longhorn

By 1900 there were about 400,000 settlers in the Oklahoma Territory and about 400,000 people in Indian Territory. People began to talk about statehood. Some Indians argued that there should be a separate Indian state. They said the Indians had been promised their own separate land "for as long as grass shall grow and rivers run."

The Indians lost the argument. Plans were made to turn the Twin Territories into one state of Oklahoma. For the Indians this meant that tribes would no longer own big pieces of land. Instead, Indian families would each own smaller pieces of land, just like the homesteaders.

On November 16, 1907 Oklahoma became our 46th state. Guthrie was the capital. Three years later, in 1910, Oklahoma City was made the capital. Do you remember those settlers who had entered Oklahoma too soon? Oklahoma was nicknamed the *Sooner State* because of them.

Remember how Coronado had come to Oklahoma in search of gold? It was found that—although it didn't have gold—the Sooner State had other treasures. Oil was one of them. You may know that oil is needed to run cars and machines. In the early 1900s oil was found in many places in the Sooner State. Oil companies set up headquarters in the city of Tulsa. Tulsa became known as the *Oil Capital of the World*.

Oil wells can be seen in many parts of Oklahoma.

Natural gas was often found near the oil. You may know that natural gas is needed to heat buildings and cook food. Oklahoma became a top producer of both oil and natural gas.

Things began to go badly for the state's farmers, however. In the 1930s the weather was terrible. There wasn't enough rain. Wind blew the soil away and caused dust storms. Part of Oklahoma was included in the region known as the *Dust Bowl*. Many Oklahoma farmers packed up and left the state.

Harvesting wheat

Those who stayed learned better ways of farming and maintaining the land. Farmers planted grass on some land to hold down the soil. They drilled wells to supply farms with water. They developed better kinds of wheat and other crops.

The United States entered World War II in 1941. Over 200,000 Oklahomans helped our country win that war. The state's farms produced food for our soldiers. Oklahoma oil also was a big help in the war effort.

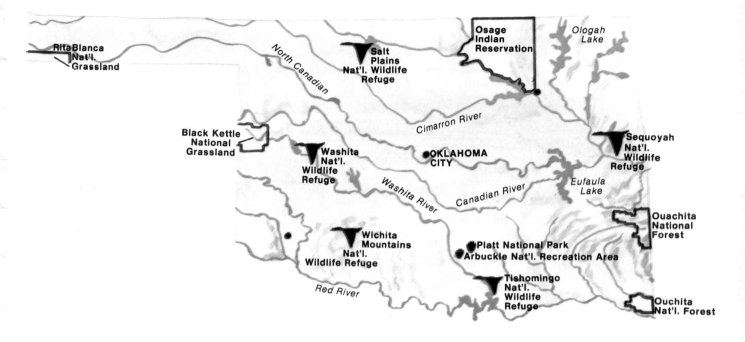

In its early days, Oklahoma had been a farming and mining state. But in the 1950s more and more factories were built. Today, manufacturing (making things in factories) is also important in Oklahoma. Machinery is the state's number one product. Oil products are made in Oklahoma. Foods are packaged in the Sooner State.

You have learned about some of Oklahoma's history. Now it is time for a trip—in words and pictures— through the Sooner State.

Oklahoma is shaped like a big, tall pan. Colorado and Kansas are neighbor states to the north. Missouri and Arkansas are to the east. Texas is to the south across the Red River. Texas and New Mexico are to the west. Look at the map. Do you see how western Oklahoma sticks out like a handle? This part of Oklahoma is called the *Panhandle.*

Pretend you are in an airplane high above Oklahoma. From the air, you can see many kinds of scenery. You can see rivers—such as the Red and the Arkansas. You can see mountain ranges—such as the Wichita and the Ouachita (WASH • e • taw) mountains. You can see grasslands where cattle graze and farmlands where crops are grown.

Your airplane is landing in a big city near the center of the state. This is Oklahoma City. Once, this area was home to Seminole and Creek Indians. The U.S.

Above: An aerial view of Oklahoma City
Left: An oil well in front of the State Capitol
building

government bought the land from the Indians in 1889. In the big run of April 22, 1889, 50,000 settlers arrived in Oklahoma City. Today, Oklahoma City is the biggest city in the state. It is also the capital of the state.

Visit the State Capitol building in Oklahoma City. Lawmakers from all across the Sooner State meet here. You can watch them as they make laws for the state. Oklahoma City is in a big oil field. You'll see oil wells right on the grounds of the Capitol building!

Above: The National Cowboy Hall of Fame
Right: *The End of the Trail* by James Earle Fraser
in the the National Cowboy Hall of Fame

Visit the National Cowboy Hall of Fame and Western
Heritage Center in Oklahoma City. There you can learn
about cowboys, Indians, and the growth of the West. If
you'd like to learn about the stars visit the Kirkpatrick
Planetarium. If you enjoy seeing animals, go to the
Oklahoma City Zoo.

Many kinds of people live in Oklahoma City. Indians
live there. There are many black people. You'll also find
people of Mexican, German, Italian, and other ethnic
backgrounds.

An art festival in Oklahoma City

Oklahoma City people work at many jobs. Quite a few work at the nearby Tinker Air Force Base. Because Oklahoma City is the state capital, a lot of the city's people work for the government. Oklahoma City people also make many products. Oil products, foods, cars, and airplanes are just four of them.

From Oklahoma City, head a short way south to Norman. The University of Oklahoma is there. Students there study to be teachers and lawyers. They study to be doctors and nurses. The University of Oklahoma is also famed for its football team. The Sooners have been the national college champs five times.

The skyline of Tulsa

About 120 miles northeast of Norman you will come to Tulsa. The city lies on the Arkansas River. A trading post was built here in 1848. Today, Tulsa is Oklahoma's second biggest city.

Hundreds of oil companies make their headquarters in the Tulsa area. A lot of machinery is made in the city. Parts of spacecraft that went to the moon were made in Tulsa.

Tulsa products go by train, truck, and plane to many cities in our country. Some go by boat on the Arkansas River.

Above: The Rose Garden at Woodward Park, Tulsa
Left: Tulsa City Hall

Have you noticed all the new buildings in Tulsa? The city's Civic Center was completed in the 1970s. The Bank of Oklahoma Tower, built in 1977, is 52 stories high.

You'll enjoy the Thomas Gilcrease Institute of American History and Art in Tulsa. You can see works by Indian artists there. This museum also has works by the Western artists Frederic Remington and Charles M. Russell. Take a look at the Creek Council Oak Tree on Cheyenne Avenue. Creek Indians once held meetings under this tree.

Many places that remind you of Indian history can be seen in Oklahoma. Sequoya's home is in far eastern Oklahoma. Sequoya, the inventor of the Cherokee alphabet, built this cabin in 1829 and lived here for 14 years. Tsa-La-Gi (JAH • LAH • GEE) Indian Village is near Tahlequah (TAHL • eh • kwa). It shows you what a Cherokee village of long ago looked like. Washita (WASH • e • taw) Battlefield is in western Oklahoma. There, General George A. Custer massacred over 100 Cheyenne Indians led by Chief Black Kettle. The American Indian Hall of Fame is at Anadarko (an • ah • DAR • ko). There you can learn about famous Indians in American history.

Today, Oklahoma has more Indians than any other state. About 120,000 Indians from at least 39 different tribes live in Oklahoma. They live in cities and towns throughout the state. Indians work at many jobs, just like other Oklahomans. There are Indians in the cattle and oil businesses. There are Indian schoolteachers, doctors, and lawyers.

Above left: A woman in Tsa-La-Gi Indian
Village weaving a basket
Above right: Kiowa gourd clan ceremonials
Bottom left: A young boy at the American Indian
Exposition in Anadarko
Bottom right: Making pottery in Tsa-La-Gi

The Indians have not forgotten their heritage. They still hold "powwows." During a powwow, Indians get together for tribal dancing and singing. A powwow is also a time to visit with old friends. "Naming ceremonies" sometimes are held by the Indian people. At these events, children and adults are given their Indian names. The "giveaway" is another custom. A giveaway might be held when an Indian completes school or comes back from the Army. The person being honored doesn't get the gifts during the giveaway. The guests do!

As you travel through Oklahoma you'll see a lot of farms and ranches. There are over five million beef cattle on the state's ranches. That means there are about twice as many beef cattle as people in the Sooner State! Oklahoma is one of our leading states for raising beef cattle.

Beef cattle

International Rodeo Finals, Tulsa

Cowboys still watch over the cattle. They brand them. Brands are marks that tell which ranch owns the cattle. Cowboys also take the cattle to market. The beef cattle are made into meat.

Cowboys today don't work only on horseback. Some ride in trucks or airplanes while they watch the cattle.

Cowboys still hold rodeos for fun. At these events, they see who can rope cattle the fastest. They see who can stay on bucking broncos the longest. Big rodeos are held at Tulsa and Oklahoma City. Buck Rutherford and Jim Shoulders are just two well-known Oklahoma rodeo champions.

Cattle are Oklahoma's main livestock product. But there are others. Chickens, hogs, and sheep are three of them.

Wheat is the main crop grown by Oklahoma farmers. Oklahoma is one of the top states for growing this grain. Today you may have eaten breakfast cereal and bread made from Oklahoma wheat.

A lot of cotton is grown in the Sooner State. Peanuts, corn, soybeans, peaches, and watermelons are other crops grown by Oklahoma farmers. Oklahoma is one of the top states for growing broomcorn. This plant isn't eaten. It's used to make brooms.

Mayo lock and dam in the Arkansas River

Do you remember how Oklahoma had dry weather during the 1930s? Periods of dry weather, called *droughts*, still hit the state. In 1980 Oklahoma was part of a large area hit by a drought. Today, there is help for farmers. In recent years many irrigation wells have been drilled to supply farms with water.

Dams on the state's rivers help supply farms with water, too. The dams hold back water and form man-made lakes. Water from these lakes is sent to farms where it is used to sprinkle crops. The dams also turn waterpower into electric power.

Fort Sill

Visit the city of Lawton, in southwestern Oklahoma. Lawton is Oklahoma's third biggest city. Beef cattle are raised near Lawton. Cotton, wheat, and peanuts are grown in the area. Car tires, clothes, and soft drinks are made in Lawton.

Fort Sill is very near Lawton. The fort was built in 1869, when the Army was trying to gain control over the Indians. The great Apache leader Geronimo spent his last years as a prisoner of war at this fort. Today, soldiers at Fort Sill learn to shoot cannons.

You'll see forests as you travel through Oklahoma. About a fifth of Oklahoma is covered by forests. Pines and oaks are two kinds of trees you'll see. Some of the trees are cut down. They are made into lumber, fence posts, and other wood products.

Above: Logging
Left: A black-tailed prairie dog

If you spend some time in Oklahoma's forests you'll see deer scooting about. Raccoons, minks, and bobcats can also be seen in the woods. Many other animals live in Oklahoma. Coyotes can be found on Oklahoma's open plains. Ranchers don't like them because they sometimes kill calves. Prairie dogs can be seen in Oklahoma, too. They aren't really dogs. They are related to squirrels. Prairie dogs live in colonies called "towns." These are tunnels in the ground. If a hungry coyote comes around, the prairie dogs hide in their tunnels.

Many birds can also be seen in Oklahoma. Quails, pheasants, and wild turkeys are just three kinds you can spot. The scissor-tailed flycatcher, which is the state bird, can be seen throughout Oklahoma.

Most everywhere you go in Oklahoma you'll see oil wells. There are about 70,000 oil wells in the Sooner State. After the oil is taken from the ground it is sent to refineries. There it is made into gasoline, heating oil, and other petroleum products.

An oil well

The Black Mesa area

Natural gas is also found in many places in the state. In the Panhandle of western Oklahoma, helium is found in the natural gas. Helium is a very light gas that is used in rocket ships and weather balloons. At a circus or zoo, you may have had your own small helium balloon.

Finish your Oklahoma trip by going to Black Mesa, in the state's northwest corner. At 4,973 feet high, Black Mesa is the highest point in the state. Once, Indians camped on Black Mesa. Their arrowheads have been found there.

Will Rogers Day celebration

Places don't tell the whole story of Oklahoma. Many interesting people have lived in the Sooner State.

Will Rogers (1879-1935) was born near the town of Oologah (OO • la • gah) when Oklahoma was still Indian Territory. He was part Cherokee. Will loved to ride a horse and do rope tricks. He became a cowboy and performed rope tricks at rodeos. While twirling his rope, Will told jokes and made funny comments about current

The annual Will Rogers Rodeo is held in Vinita.

events. People laughed, but they also thought that there was a lot of wisdom in what he said. Will Rogers became a famous humorist. He made movies and radio shows. He wrote books and had his own newspaper column. One of Will Rogers' most famous remarks was: "I never met a man I didn't like." The "Cowboy Philosopher" died in a plane crash in 1935.

A statue of Jim Thorpe
in the American
Indian Hall of Fame

Jim Thorpe (1886-1953) was an Oklahoma Indian who was born near the town of Prague (PRAHG). Jim could ride a horse at three years of age. He could swim soon after that. Jim Thorpe became an athlete. He could do just about everything in sports. He was a star college football player. He won two events in the 1912 Olympics. Jim Thorpe played major league baseball *and* pro football. Many sports experts call Jim Thorpe the greatest American athlete of all time.

The great raft race is held annually on the Arkansas River.

Oklahoma has produced many great baseball players. Mickey Mantle was born in Spavinaw (SPAV • eh • no) in 1931. As a boy, Mickey sometimes played baseball 12 hours a day. All that practice paid off! As a big leaguer, Mantle hit 536 home runs for the New York Yankees. He played in 12 World Series. His 18 home runs in World Series is a record. His 40 runs driven in during the World Series is also a record. Carl Hubbell, Willie Stargell, and Johnny Bench are three other great ballplayers from Oklahoma.

In Tsa-La-Gi, dance is part of the recreation of the Trail of Tears.

Maria Tallchief was born in Fairfax in 1925. She is part Osage Indian. As a child, Maria watched tribal dancing. She took dancing lessons. Later, Maria Tallchief became a famous ballet dancer.

Leroy Gordon Cooper, Jr. was born in Shawnee in 1927. When Leroy was just eight years old, he was sometimes allowed to take the controls of his dad's airplane. Later, Cooper became an astronaut. Then he flew really far! Cooper was the first man to orbit the Earth in two separate flights. Thomas Stafford, born in Weatherford in 1930, is another famous Oklahoma astronaut.

Left: The highest
spot in
Oklahoma is
4,973 feet.
Right: Martin
Park in
Oklahoma City

The great folk singer Woody Guthrie (1912-1967) was born in Okemah (oh • KEE • mah). While still a teenager, he started roaming across the United States. He made up songs about the people and places he saw. Guthrie wrote songs about poor farm workers. He wrote songs about the beauty of our country. "This Land is Your Land" and "Blowing Down This Old Dusty Road" are just two of the songs Woody Guthrie wrote and sang.

The great black writer Ralph Ellison was born in Oklahoma City in 1914. *Invisible Man,* his novel about a young black man, won the National Book Award in 1953.

Chester Gould was born in Pawnee in 1900. As a boy, he loved to draw cartoons. He later created the famous comic strip, *Dick Tracy.*

Turner Falls

Carl Albert was born in McAlester (mick • AL • eh • ster) in 1908. He became a lawyer. Oklahomans elected him to the U.S. Congress in 1946. Carl Albert became one of our country's most important lawmakers. From 1971 to 1977 he was speaker of the United States House of Representatives.

Home to Sequoya . . . Will Rogers . . . Jim Thorpe . . . and Mickey Mantle.

A state where the Five Civilized Tribes settled . . . and where thousands of settlers arrived in big land runs.

Now a leading state for oil . . . natural gas . . . beef cattle . . . and wheat.

This is the Sooner State—Oklahoma!

Facts About OKLAHOMA

Area—69,919 square miles (18th biggest state)

Greatest Distance North to South—230 miles

Greatest Distance East to West—464 miles

Border States—Colorado and Kansas to the north; Missouri and Arkansas to the east; Texas to the south; Texas and New Mexico to the west

Highest Point—4,973 feet above sea level (Black Mesa)

Lowest Point—287 feet above sea level (on the Little River)

Hottest Recorded Temperature—120°

Coldest Recorded Temperature—Minus 27°

Statehood—Our 46th state, on November 16, 1907

Origin of Name—The word *Oklahoma* comes from the Choctaw Indian language; it means *land of the red people*

Capital—Oklahoma City (since 1910)

Previous Capital—Guthrie

Counties—77

U.S. Senators—2

U.S. Representatives—6

State Senators—48

State Representatives—101

State Song—"Oklahoma!" by Richard Rodgers and Oscar Hammerstein II

State Motto—*Labor Omnia Vincit* (Latin, meaning "Labor Conquers All Things")

Nicknames—The Sooner State, the Boomer State

State Seal—Adopted in 1907

State Flag—Adopted in 1925

State Flower—Mistletoe

State Bird—Scissor-tailed flycatcher

State Animal—Bison
State Reptile—Mountain boomer lizard
State Fish—White bass
State Grass—Indiangrass
State Tree—Redbud
State Colors—Green and white
Some Rivers—Arkansas, Canadian, Verdigris, Cimarron, Neosho, Red,
    Kiamichi, Washita, Little
Lakes—About 100 natural ones and over 200 man-made ones
Mountain Ranges—Arbuckle, Ouachita, Wichita, Ozarks
Wildlife—Deer, raccoons, minks, bobcats, coyotes, prairie dogs, opossums,
    otters, squirrels, rabbits, rattlesnakes and other snakes, robins, scissor-
    tailed flycatchers, quails, prairie chickens, pheasants, wild turkeys, many
    other kinds of birds
Farm Products—Beef cattle, hogs, sheep, chickens, eggs, wheat, cotton,
    peanuts, soybeans, corn, broomcorn, peaches, watermelons, barley, oats
Mining—Oil, natural gas, helium, coal, copper, granite
Manufacturing—Machinery, petroleum products, packaged foods,
    wood products, plastic products, aircraft and other transportation
    equipment
Population—1980 census: 3,025,495 (1989 estimate: 3,329,961)

Major Cities	1980 Census	1989 Estimate
Oklahoma City	404,014	461,844
Tulsa	360,919	392,720
Lawton	80,054	86,483
Norman	68,020	86,285
Enid	50,363	52,267
Midwest City	49,559	54,873
Muskogee	40,011	44,835

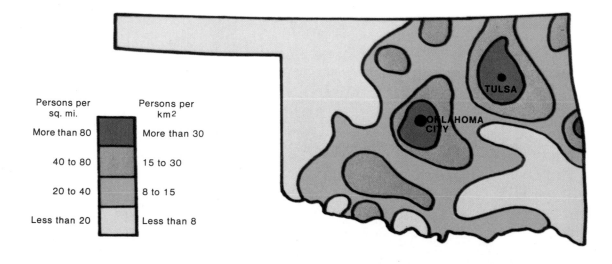

Persons per sq. mi.	Persons per km2
More than 80	More than 30
40 to 80	15 to 30
20 to 40	8 to 15
Less than 20	Less than 8

Oklahoma History

People first came to Oklahoma at least 9,000 years ago.

1541—Francisco Vásquez de Coronado of Spain crosses Oklahoma while searching for gold

1682—La Salle claims a large area, including Oklahoma, for France

1762—Spain takes control of Oklahoma

1800—France regains control

1803—As part of the Louisiana Purchase, the United States buys Oklahoma from France

1820-1842—The Choctaw, Creek, Chickasaw, Cherokee, and Seminole Indians are moved to what is called Indian Territory

1824—U.S. government builds Fort Gibson and Fort Towson

1844—Cherokee print Oklahoma's first newspaper, the *Cherokee Advocate,* at Tahlequah

1861-1865—During the Civil War, many Indians side with the South

1870-1872—Oklahoma's first railroad—the Missouri-Kansas-Texas Railroad—is built

1872—Coal mining begins in Oklahoma

1879—"Boomers" try to settle in Oklahoma

1889—After the United States opens part of Oklahoma for settlement, 50,000 people arrive there on April 22

1890—Territory of Oklahoma is created; this and the Indian Territory are called the "Twin Territories"

1892—University of Oklahoma opens

1893—In the biggest of Oklahoma's land runs, over 100,000 settlers arrive on September 16

1900—There are about 400,000 people in the Territory of Oklahoma and about 400,000 in Indian Territory

1905—The Indians try to create their own separate state, but aren't successful

1907—On November 16, Oklahoma becomes our 46th state; Guthrie is the capital

1910—Oklahoma City becomes the capital

1917-1918—After the United States enters World War I, over 88,000 Oklahomans are in uniform

1920—Beginning of great production from Osage County oil fields

1928—Oklahoma City oil field begins producing

1930s—Great Depression and dust storms hit Oklahoma

1933—The famous Oklahoma airplane pilot Wiley Post becomes the first person to fly around the world alone

1935—Wiley Post and the great cowboy-humorist Will Rogers are killed in an Alaska plane crash

1937—Work begins on the Grand River Dam in eastern Oklahoma

1941-1945—After the United States enters World War II, over 200,000 Oklahomans serve; Oklahoma oil also helps the war effort

1950—Population of the Sooner State is 2,233,351

1953—The Turner Turnpike, going from Oklahoma City to Tulsa, is finished

1955—Oklahoma City is chosen to be the home of the National Cowboy Hall of Fame

1970—The Arkansas River Navigation System is completed

1971—Mrs. Patience Latting becomes Oklahoma City's first woman mayor

1973—Big prison riot at McAlester

1974—Oklahomans elect their youngest governor ever—35-year-old David L. Boren

1977—The 52-story Bank of Oklahoma Tower and the Tulsa Performing Arts Center are completed in Tulsa

1980—Oklahoma is part of a large area hit by drought

1983—George P. Nigh is reelected governor for a second term

1984—An inundation, caused by a twelve-inch rainfall that forced rivers and creeks to overflow, becomes the worst disaster in Tulsa's history

1985—Wilma Mankiller is sworn in as Principal Chief of the Cherokee Nation of Oklahoma—the first woman in history to lead a major American Indian tribe

1987—Henry Bellmon begins first term as governor; over 100 banks close in the state because of a nationwide depression in the oil industry

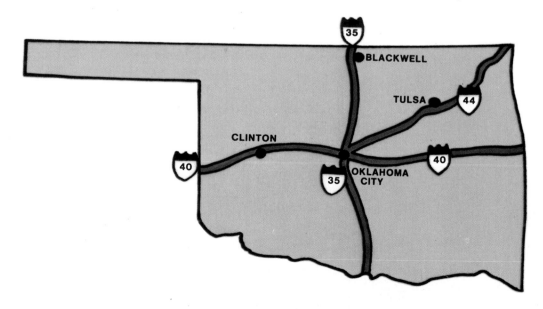

INDEX

About the Author:

Dennis Fradin attended Northwestern University on a creative writing scholarship and was graduated in 1967. While still at Northwestern, he published his first stories in *Ingenue* magazine and also won a prize in *Seventeen's* short story competition. A prolific writer, Dennis Fradin has been regularly publishing stories in such diverse places as *The Saturday Evening Post, Scholastic, National Humane Review, Midwest,* and *The Teaching Paper.* He has also scripted several educational films. Since 1970 he has taught second grade reading in a Chicago school—a rewarding job, which, the author says, "provides a captive audience on whom I test my children's stories." Married and the father of three children, Dennis Fradin spends his free time with his family or playing a myriad of sports and games with his childhood chums.

About the Artists:

Len Meents studied painting and drawing at Southern Illinois University and after graduation in 1969 he moved to Chicago. Mr. Meents works full time as a painter and illustrator. He and his wife and child currently make their home in LaGrange, Illinois.

Richard Wahl, graduate of the Art Center College of Design in Los Angeles, has illustrated a number of magazine articles and booklets. He is a skilled artist and photographer who advocates realistic interpretations of his subjects. He lives with his wife and two sons in Libertyville, Illinois.